No One Cares What You Had for Lunch

100 Ideas for Your Blog

Margaret Mason

Peachpit Press

No One Cares What You Had for Lunch: 100 Ideas for Your Blog
Margaret Mason

Peachpit Press
1249 Eighth Street
Berkeley, CA 94710
510/524-2178
800/293-9444
510/524-2221 (fax)

Find us on the Web at www.peachpit.com
To report errors, please send a note to errata@peachpit.com

Peachpit Press is a division of Pearson Education

Acquisitions Editor: Michael Nolan
Editor: Ted Waitt
Production Editor: Lupe Edgar
Illustrations: Tiffany Larsen
Interior Design: Charlene Charles-Will
Compositor: Interactive Composition Corporation
Indexer: James Minkin
Cover Design: Charlene Charles-Will
Cover Image: Veer Images

ISBN 0-321-44972-X

9 8 7 6 5 4 3 2 1

Printed and bound in the United States of America

You are great.

Maggie Mason

Winter Reading List

- Twilight books
- Hang-overs from summer reading list
- What color is your parachute
- Royal spyness

E, TED
ON
VEN
RA
IMBERLIE
HAEL
A
, BARRY
N F.
RLES.
M
ON, WENDY
NK JR.
TER
AIMEE
, JENNIFER
NN
HN
NANCY
EITH
MARK
ERIC
R, RENEE
AVID
, JENNIFER
SYLVIA
SSICA
OBERT
, SEAN
RON P
IDRA
JENNIFER
ARL
, MARK
ATTHEW
DA
H, VALERIE

___ REIS, JAMES
___ REOHR, CHRISTOPHER
___ REUSS, CAROLINE
___ RICHARDS, PRISCILLA
___ RITCHEY, JAIME
___ ROBERTS, BARRY
___ ROETH, JACQUES
___ ROOD, THOMAS
___ ROSE, ALLISON
___ ROSENBERG, PAULA
___ RUDER, ADAM
___ RUSSEELL, BETH
___ RUSSELL, NATHAN
___ RUTH, MARCIA
___ SAINTCROSS, JOHN
___ SALISBURY. MICHELLE
___ SAUNDERS, HEATHER
___ SAUVIE, MARY
___ SAVAGE, KATHLEEN
___ SAVIO, PETER
___ SCHUCKER, ERIN
___ SERBU, RENEE
___ SGROI, CHRISTOPHER
___SHAUGER, JENNIFER
___SCHILLER, RICHARD
___ SHIMAZU; MICHAEL
___ SILLETTI, JORDAN
___ SMITH, CHRISTOPHER
___ SMITH, SCOTT
___ SOVIE, MICHELE
___ STACEY, DIANE
___ STASACK, JUDITH
___ STERLING, REBECCA
___ STEVENS, AMANDA
___ STUMP, CHRISTOPHER
___ SULLIVAN, JOANNE
___ TARIO, JOSEPH
___ TIGHE, ANDREW
___ TORPEY, MARK

FOR YOUR

___ SIGNATURE
___ APPROVAL
___ INFORMATION
___ COMMENTS
___ FILES
___ DIRECT HANDLING
___ PLEASE RETURN
___ OTHER

____

____

Blog Posts

Tonight → Too Busy
→ Busy summer; looking forward to more downtime in the fall

Tomorrow → Yeay for fall
→ talk abt. back yard projects
chopping/splitting wood
mulching trees?
→ front yard landscaping
→ pumpkin pies + corn maze

Tommorow night → wood chipping trees

Sunday → football and fall food favorites (mom's beef stew)?

Next week → house painting projects (awning, red walls)

→ dormer days
14 feet, planning the space, woke up freaking out abt the closet

closet

bathroom → paint choices (originally orange) and shower curtain

726 Exchange Street, Suite 821
Buffalo, NY 14210
www.nyserda.org
p.:(716) 842-1522 x3037
f.: (716) 842-0156
e.: sls@nyserda.org

Let Them Eat Cake!

I did; and there was no revolt.
Imagine that. Maybe someone
should have told Marie Antoinette
that if you *give* people cake -
they tend to be much happier.
↳ talk alot cake at family picnic.

Fun fact/
Side note - 7th grade French class -
first thing we did was pick our French
'Names'. I chose Antoinette because I
really liked it. ... for all of about 10
minutes until I learned that Marie Antoinette
was beheaded! Then not so much but it
was too late. I was stuck with it for a
whole year. Next September tho I was
quick to switch - I chose Lisette after that
since I was already used to answering to
it [link to nickname post] and it didn't bear any
negative connotations.

	DATE RECEIVED	INSTALLER
189	11/03/08	John Wright (HVCE)
190	11/03/08	Renewable Power Systems (M
191	11/03/08	Hudson Valley Clean Energy (
192	11/03/08	Solar Generation, Inc (T. Koel
193	11/03/08	Solar Generation, Inc (J. Spiott
194	11/03/08	Solar Generation, Inc (J. Spiott
195	11/03/08	Damiani and Sun, Inc (C.
196	11/03/08	ISI Solar (J. Albert)
197	10/30/08	Global Resource Options (D. K
198	11/05/08	O'Connell Electric Company (
199	11/05/08	Renewable Power Systems (
200	11/06/08	Mercury Solar Systems (A. Co
201	11/06/08	Aeon Solar (Rob Ashmore)
202	11/06/08	Mercury Solar Systems (A. Cos
203	11/06/08	O'Connell Electric Company (
204	11/7/08	Aeon Solar (Rob Ashmore)
205	11/7/08	Hudson Valley Clean Energy (J.
206	11/7/08	Hudson Valley Clean Energy (J.
207	11/7/08	Hudson Valley Clean Energy (J.
	[illegible]/08	Renewable Power Systems (M. S
		[illegible]

Life is all about the little things, right?
I was thinking this morning how many little things I encounter on a daily basis that make me smile/laugh to myself/improve my mood. Often time I don't really give these things much thought, but life is made up of all these things and years from now I'd like to remember what made up my days

There's part of a sign - I don't know what the whole thing is supposed to say. but it says 'lets' and every time I see it* I think of my sister (which is every day at work) as a High School Cheerleader Chanting "Lets go, lets go L-e-t-s-g-o!"

Fruit snacks - recently I am obsessed with them; I can't get enough!

A text from people I care about - always makes me smile

A great song on the radio on the way to work (better yet; a series of them the whole way in!)

Seeing the sunrise/sunset depending on the season

__ CAPELLO, ALLISON
__ CAPORALE, SHANNON
__ CARVER, ROBERT
__ CHAVALLI, JAYASREE
__ CHAVES, LAURA
__ CHICK, MARY
__ CLARK, LORI
__ COLELLO, VICKI
__ COLL, CHRISTOPHER
__ COSTELLO, PETER
__ COUP, DAVE
__ COX, ASHLEY
__ CUNNINGHAM, TAMMY
__ CUSHING, JUSTIN
__ DARE, MARILYN
__ DARLING, DOREEN
__ DAVIDSON, MARGARET
__ DAWSON, CHARLE-PAN
__ DECKER, MARK
__ DENMAN, EMILY
__ DEROSA, JOSEPH
__ DERUSSO, ALICIA
__ DESIMONE,TRACEY
__ DEVINE, HOPE
X DOOLEY, KATHLEEN
__ DOUGLAS, PETER
__ DRAKE, RICHARD
__ EARLEY, CHERYL
__ EARLEY, MARCIA
__ EBERTS, JEANELLE
__ EGGERS, MARK
__ ELVIN, MARGARET
__ ENGEL, VICTORIA
__ FARRELL, DANIEL
__ FERRANTI, ADELE
__ FIANO, MICHELLE
__ FIESINGER, THOMAS
__ FINKLE, STEVEN
__ FITZGERALD, PATRICK

__ KEEGAN, MARYFRANCIS
__ KENDALL, JILL
__ KENNEDY, MICHELE
__ KERAGA, KELVIN
__ KHOSROVA, MITCHELL
__ KIM, HELEN
__ KING, TRICIA
__ KLOPFER, CYNTHIA
__ KNEELAND, CRAIG
__ LABARR, ALAN
__ LAMPMAN, GREGORY
__ LARSEN, SCOTT
__ LAWRENCE, TED
__ LA VADA, DON
__ LEBEL, STEVEN
__ LECAIN, SARA
__ LENIHAN, KIMBERLIE
__ LEVY, DANA
__ LIEBOWITZ, BARRY
__ LOVE, JOHN F.
__ LUKE, CHARLES.
__ LYNCH, TOM
__ MACE, FRANK JR.
__ MAHAR, PETER
__ MALLORY, AIMEE
__ MANIERRE, JENNIFER
__ MARTIN, JOHN
__ MARUCCI, NANCY
__ MAS, CARL
__ MAURER, KEITH
__ MAYHEW, MARK
__ MAZZONE, ERIC
__ MCALLISTER, RENEE
__ MCCABE, DAVID
__ MCDONALD, JENNIFER
__ MCGAHAY, SYLVIA
__ MCKEE, JESSICA
__ MCMULLEN, SEAN
MCNAB. DARON P

__ RICHARDS, PRISCILLA
__ RITCHEY, JAIME
__ ROBERTS, BARRY
__ ROSENBERG, PAULA
__ RUDER, ADAM
__ RUSSELL, BETH
__ RUSSELL, NATHAN
__ RUTH, MARCIA
__ RYAN, COLLEEN
__ SAINTCROSS, JOHN
__ SAUNDERS, HEATHER
__ SAUVIE, MARY
__ SAVAGE, KATHLEEN
__ SAVIO, PETER
__ SCHUCKER, ERIN
__ SERBU, RENEE
__ SHIMAZU, MICHAEL
__ SMITH, SCOTT
__ SOVIE, MICHELE
__ STACEY, DIANE
__ STASACK, JUDITH
__ STEVENS, AMANDA
__ STUMP, CHRISTOPHER
__ SULLIVAN, JOANNE
__ TARIO, JOSEPH
__ TIGHE, ANDREW
__ TORPEY, MARK
__ TRANT, JILL
__ TRAVISON, ANN
__ TREANOR, BRIAN M.
__ TUERS, THERESE
__ VANGORDER, ANDREW
__ VILLENEUVE, KAREN
__ VISCUSI, ROSEANNE
__ WAGNER, JOE
__ WALSH, JACLYN
__ WALTON, MARSHA
__ WASHINGTON, LISA
WATSON. MARK

Not so favorite Meals

Cheese Rarebit
Chipped Beef
Regular meat loaf
Mac+ Cheese w/HDs

Yummy

- Sausages + Acorn squash
- Apple + corn fritters
- The good meatloaf
- Chicken+ broccoli braid
- Mac + Cheese
- Teriyaki steak
- DDPC
- Home made pizza (grilled Pizza)
- Popcorn + apples
- PB Pizzas
- Beef stew + home made bread
- Corn Chowder (w/bacon)
- Summer Chicken salad w/mandarine oranges + Lemon yogurt sauce

Sides

The sweet potatoes
Thanksgiving green beans

July 25-31, 2011
Weekly Love Horoscope for Cancer

You have the power to lure, persuade and bewitch. Take a chance and see where (and who) it gets you. Don't let past failures overshadow you. Don't imagine your next lover will be a continuation of your ex. And if you're looking for a life partner, don't map out every step of a dance that hasn't even begun. Staying confident and present turns any date into an adventure. Cultivate this quality and they will be lining up to be with you!

Dedication

For my husband, Bryan Mason, who is far superior to all other husbands, and indeed better than most people of all sorts.

Contents

CHAPTER 1

CHAPTER 2

CHAPTER 3

CHAPTER 4

CHAPTER 5

Introduction

Jacob likes: music, movies, pepperoni pizza, and hanging out with friends. Shelly spends more time with parakeets than most. Today, Beth went to work, came home, watched *The Daily Show* (which was way hilarious, btw), and had a Jenny Craig Island Chicken meal (which was decent, btw).

Have your eyes glazed over yet? Yeah, mine too.

The popularity of blogging amazes and inspires me. Here are *millions* of people who've found a format that makes them eager to publish. For many bloggers, their sites are the first place they've voluntarily written or produced a project in their lives. This is huge! It's a Renaissance in personal expression! It's an astonishing historical record! It's the voice of an entire people! It's an awesome way to K.I.T.!

So why aren't English teachers high-fiving each other in the streets? Well, let's examine that first post more closely:

> Hello, world!

Okay. And the second?

> I had a cheese sandwich today. It was delicious.

Mmm hmm.... The third?

> I don't know what to write about.

I see.

So my theory is this. Like any endeavor, you make a choice when you start a blog. You either put in some effort to make something engaging and creative that builds community, or you toss a "me too" onto the growing pile of repetitive, navel-gazing content.

So how do you avoid me-too syndrome? Well, the answer is conveniently located right here in your hands. *No One Cares What You Had for Lunch* gives you the inspiration you need to create posts that keep visitors coming back. Use the hundred suggestions to stock your blog with fresh content and help make blogging fun again. Your site will rock so hard that you will gaze upon your typing fingers in wonder.

Before we get to it, I have a few people to thank. First, thanks to my imprudently supportive husband, Bryan Mason. Thanks to the long-time readers of Mighty Girl and Mighty Goods—you guys rock me like the proverbial hurricane. Thanks to Jeffrey Veen for helping me find a publisher; my editor, Ted Waitt, for guiding me through a rigorous production schedule; Jesse James Garrett for his always prudent advice; Evan Williams for making the tool that introduced me to blogging; Allison Post Harris, Patricia Marchetti, and Heather Armstrong for offering shoulders to vent on; Andrew Womack, Rosecrans Baldwin, and the entire team at The Morning News for welcoming me into a community of inspiring writers; Tiffany Larsen, who always has an ideal illustration when I need one; and the deskies who are easily distracted and always helpful. Lastly, thanks to Ritual Roasters for your delicious rose-petal tea and tasty open wireless network.

Now, let's get to work.

1

Fifteen Minutes to Fame

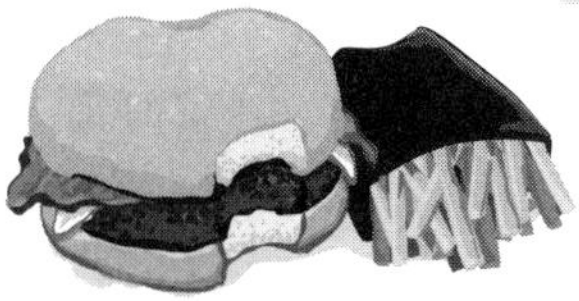

You have a mean case of blogger's block, and only a few minutes to post. These quick ideas will help you come up with quality entries, toot sweet.

1 | Reign supreme.

Your cousin wears a red dress to your grandmother's funeral. The guy in the Porsche takes up two spaces at the front of the lot. Your boss enjoys scheduling meetings so she can arrive thirty minutes late.

All of us should just learn to tolerate stupid people. But what if we didn't have to? If you ruled the world, things would be better, at least in a few small ways. Heather Powazek Champ (www.hchamp.com), for example, has distinct opinions on how you should be hanging your toilet paper.

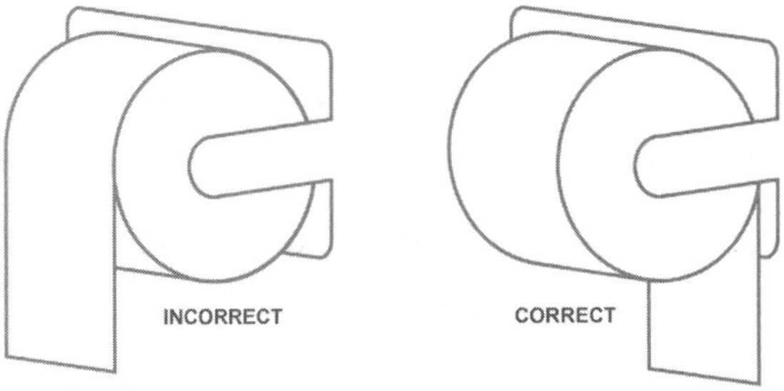

When I am queen, I shall decree that all rolls of toilet paper be correctly inserted into the toilet paper dispensers. Correctly? You have all been improperly instructed to place your toilet paper with the "tongue" facing outward. This is incorrect. Why? It's ugly. Please view the illustration above. Isn't the arrangement on the right far more aesthetically pleasing than that on the left? But what about ease of use, you ask? I don't give a rat's ass about ease of use. I want the world to be a more beautiful place, and I'm going to start with your toilet paper. Thank you.

2 | Fess up.

Writing gives you time to consider how to present yourself. Online, you can be smarter, wittier, kinder. Alternately, you can be a mind-numbing bore. This sometimes happens because your audience (however small you think it may be) gives you stage fright. You worry that certain things could be misconstrued, so you're tempted to water things down. You hone, delete, and reshape until you've sucked all the juice from your posts.

All readers need an occasional dose of schadenfreude, so fess up. How do you fail? Do you consistently kill plants? Keep getting fired? Always take the last cookie? That's the stuff, friends. To err is human, but to share? Divine.

3 | Give us something.

Tell your readers about the presents you'll remember forever. Andrea Scher of Superhero Journal (www.superherodesigns.com) wrote about a few of the best gifts she'd ever given or gotten. A couple of standouts:

> WISH CONTAINERS I love putting wishes, lists, worries, and things I'd like to manifest in a cigar box. Some call it a "God box." I call it the pneumatic tube (like the old fashioned bank deposit containers). [My friend] Sasha made me a portable tube in the form of a hand-bound book. She painted on several pages, and glued tiny envelopes inside to place wishes. This book is my portable wish container for the most tender things.
>
> TRIBUTE BOOKS The best gift I have ever given was a book that I made for my mom for Mother's Day. I asked each of our family members and several of her old friends to answer three important questions: 1. How did you meet my mom? 2. Choose one word to describe her. 3. What do you love most about her?
>
> What I got back were incredible stories (things I had never known about my mom), gorgeous old photographs, and poignant declarations of love from family and friends. It was truly one of those presents that was a gift not only to her, but to everyone who contributed to it.

4 | Exploit the youth.

Turn away from your monitor, and hunker down with the Legos. Why be a parent—or a cousin, or an aunt, or an uncle—if not to exploit children for blog content? Kids are hilarious and surprisingly insightful. A quick conversation with a five-year-old will yield a dozen more amusing moments than you could call to mind by banging your head against the keyboard. Witness this conversation with my then three-year-old nephew, Trevor:

> Me: What do pigs say?
>
> Trevor: ...ahh.... Oink! Oink!
>
> Me: What do dogs say?
>
> Trevor: Bark! Bark!
>
> Me: What do elephants say?
>
> Trevor: ...aaah.... Prrrrrbt!
>
> Me: What do Trevors say?
>
> Trevor: PLEASE!

5 | Be a sage.

People love to tell you what to do with your life. You're graduating, getting married, having a kid—whatever it is, they have some advice. Do you know a great advice giver, or better yet, someone who's prone to making inappropriate suggestions?

Think through all the counsel you've gotten over the years. What opinions have people offered that stuck with you, whether they turned out to be on the money or completely nuts?

If you'd rather be the one to tell other people what to do, offer readers your hard-learned lessons—satirical or solemn.

6 | Count your blessings.

Your blog is such an excellent place to gripe that you may be tempted to grouse full time. If you start to feel surly just sitting down to your keyboard, it's time to mix things up. Think about what's going right in your life, in your day, or just in general. Try listing a few things you're glad about. Eventually, you may find that you could dedicate an entire section of your site to stuff that makes you happy.

Here's what went right for me on a recent Sunday morning:

- We woke up early, got dressed, and went outside.
- It was sunny and warm for the first time in ages, and *The New York Times* was on the stoop.
- We climbed in our little orange car, and drove for breakfast.
- There was a metered parking spot right out front.
- We didn't have to plug the meter, because it was Sunday.
- There was no wait for the table.
- The coffee came right away.
- There was melted cheese.
- Amongst all the grape jellies, there was one strawberry left.

7 | Examine your paperwork.

In 2001, Sarah Brown (www.queserasera.org) began sending weekly emails to her friends that contained the most agonizing excerpts from her old diaries. That effort became Cringe, a monthly reading series based on the same premise.

In celebration of adolescence, type in some of your old journal entries—or better yet, post a photo. Did you keep any notes your best friend passed you in fourth period? Those are equally golden.

If you're timid about baring your downy, flightless thirteen-year-old soul, Sarah offers this guideline: "When you read it to yourself, do you physically cringe? Then it's funny."

Is there any youthful foible too mortifying for even Sarah to share? Yes, in fact:

> One time, way before my first kiss, I filled an entire notebook with pirate love stories. Featuring me. And Christian Bale. I had seen some TV version of *Treasure Island* starring Christian Bale, who I'd been hot for ever since *Empire of the Sun*.... The only way you knew there were pirates was that they prefaced every sentence with "aye." It was so, so bad. So bad that I would still be embarrassed to even let my dearest friends, the ones who've seen me naked and snotty and unwashed, see it. In fact, if I suddenly die, [my friend] Josh has instructions to go find the yellow notebook and burn it, sight unseen.

8 | Talk back.

You can use your blog as a forum to say whatever you like, or you can start a conversation. If you read or see something that gets you thinking—on another site, in a magazine, on TV, anywhere—respond on your blog. This can be especially satisfying when something annoys you, but you can also second an unpopular opinion or add your voice to a topic that deserves more attention. Occasionally, you'll find that your readers will also have something to say, and will leave comments or continue the discussion on their own sites.

9 | Transform yourself.

You've painted wasabi on your nails to keep from nibbling. You've set up Web calendars with email alerts to help you remember your mom's birthday. You keep promising yourself that one day you'll just dump the TV that sucks up your time.

Being good is hard, and hardly worth the effort. But what if you could just wish away a few of your bad habits? Which annoying personal tics would you choose? And while you're at it, are there any good habits you'd like to magically adopt?

10 | Get nostalgic.

You're a grown-up now, or close enough anyway—taxes loom, you book your own dental appointments, and you no longer break up with people by ignoring them. (Right?) Now that you're here, what reminds you of your youth? Maybe you miss swing sets, or eating french fries without a fleeting prayer for your arteries. Whether you long for animal crackers or the unstructured time you had when you were a student, tell us what takes you back.

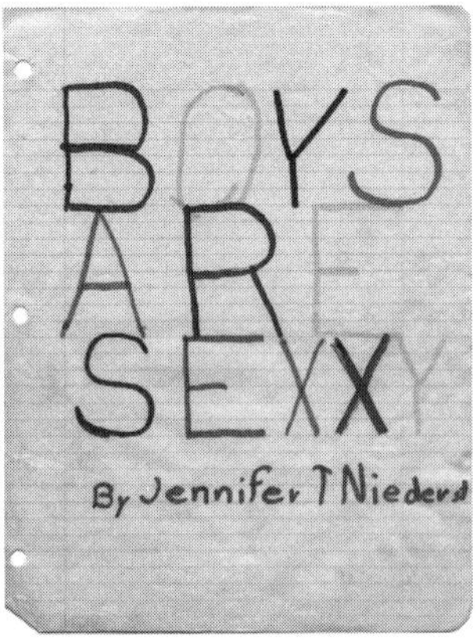

Designer and author Jennifer Niederst Robbins (www.jenville.com) often posts bits of her past, including '80s photos of New Wave Jen, a short audio clip of her five-year-old self singing Ray Dorset's "In the Summertime," and scans of books she created as a kid, including this copy of the classic *Boys Are Sexxy.*

11 | Curate the Web.

If you have a mean case of writer's block, one of the most valuable things you can do on the Web is to help edit it. When it feels like nothing exciting is happening in your life, help readers find quality content by quoting a superior post from someone else's blog and then linking through to it. I sometimes set up posts like this when I'm going on vacation, so readers have somewhere to go for fresh content. The sneak preview also encourages people to explore, and possibly discover a new site to add to their blogrolls.

12 | Play favorites.

There's nothing wrong with offering recommendations, but it's possible that the world could live without another extended review of *The Godfather*. If you don't have time for a full-blown analysis, or if it just seems unnecessary, consider starting a brief list of the media you think readers should check out. Just name a few of the movies, books, magazines, or songs that have affected you.

You can keep it simple by calling out your top three in a given category—and maybe adding a sentence to explain the more obscure selections—or you can make running lists to update whenever you come across something noteworthy.

Jason Kottke (www.kottke.org) does an impressive job of tracking the media he consumes on separate pages of his site. For movies (www.kottke.org/movies), he offers ratings, and a review here and there. For books (www.kottke.org/books), he displays thumbnails of the covers and offers a review of each. By organizing his picks so thoughtfully, he's created a deep resource, one post at a time.

13 | Act on ceremony.

My friend Rachel bakes a cake every year at Christmas so her family can sing happy birthday to Jesus. On Independence Day, my family gathers in the street to do interpretive dance with sparklers. Some families are strict about traditions, passing them to each new generation. And sometimes individuals create their own rituals.

What are the family traditions or personal rituals you practice? How have they evolved over the years? Are there any new traditions you've always wanted to introduce?

14 | Watch your language.

What are the words you love, or the phrases you wish would come back in fashion? On my blog, I've requested that everyone adopt the following:

- "I don't give a tinker's damn."
- "Here's mud in your eye!"
- "He's a tall, cool drink of water."

My readers are pulling for:

- "Bangarang!"
- "I like the cut of his jib."
- "I'll fix your little red wagon."

I'm guessing you're a "Boy, howdy!" type, but there's no telling until you weigh in.

15 | Fill the gaps.

Use memory triggers to help you generate interesting stories. Find a photo you love, upload it, and describe everything you remember about it being taken. Or look through your library and think about where you read a particular book. There are things all around you that can help you piece together anecdotes. You can even think about smells that remind you of other places and times, or textures and sounds that take you back.

16 | Mine consumer culture.

All of us are picky about something. Say you've become a little obsessed in your quest for the perfect oven mitt, or you lie awake at night wondering whether it's even *possible* for lip gloss to be shiny enough without feeling sticky. Once in a while we stumble on something that's just right, and we want to tell everyone we know. What are the items, ideas, or resources that improve your life?

Kevin Kelly, co-founder of *Wired* magazine, developed his Cool Tools site (www.kk.org/cooltools) to help readers share useful information about the things they love.

Readers have suggested using Velcro plant ties for tidying electrical cables. They've also flagged abuse-resistant cell phones, and located a device that turns the top of your toilet tank into a sink. Ah, the many faces of convenience.

17 | Dial a post.

Years ago, my niece Emma left a message on my voicemail: "Auntie Mahget! I lost a toof!" I teared up when I heard it, and saved her message. Then I saved the one where my friend Jenny told me she was pregnant, and the one where my husband called me drunk from a friend's bachelor party, and so on.

Soon enough, my voicemail was full, but I couldn't bear to part with my collection. I headed over to Odeo Studio (http://studio.odeo.com) and converted those messages into podcasts.

If podcasting seems like too much effort, you can always use the same principle for your best text messages.

18 | Spill everything.

When you throw a party, at least one person will open your medicine cabinet to find your athlete's foot medication. If you think bookshelves and CD racks are revealing, try going through someone's laptop bag. The most interesting spaces are the ones we never inspect. Most people don't even know what they have in their own wallet. Do you? Catalog the contents of a space that isn't ordinarily open to the public.

Yahoo's photo-sharing service, Flickr (www.flickr.com), has a huge tag group based on what's in people's bags. They label relevant photos with the tag *whatsinmybag*.

Here are the highlights from Flickr Co-Founder Caterina Fake's bag:

- Canadian passport
- American passport
- My birth certificate. My passport is expired, so I need to carry this around to cross borders.
- Pencil from the Hotel San Jose in Austin, Texas, where I stayed during SxSW in 2001.
- Earplugs
- More earplugs. I'm really sensitive to noise and have been sleeping in strange places—hotels with protesters across the street, planes, and in office space here at Digifoo.
- Tiny, tiny, beautiful, earth-tone Post-It notes for marking books, that I got at Muji in Tokyo.

19 | Give us your scraps.

Most people have a rough system for saving good ideas. Do you rip pages from magazines, collect quotations, or hoard business cards with particularly good designs? If you're bothering to save that stuff, someone else will want to see it too.

When I'm finished reading a book, I pull all the passages I've underlined and post them on my site. It helps me remember why I loved a book, and tells my readers whether they might like it too.

I was looking into the nuances of semicolon usage when I came across this gem in *The Chicago Manual of Style*, 14th edition:

> Mittelbach had forgotten his reeds; hence he was prevented from jamming with the others.

20 | Make us gasp.

A skipping stone, a shrill two-finger whistle—kids are easily impressed. Once you're a little older, amazement is harder to come by. It takes something really spectacular. You know, like a ludicrously fluffy angora rabbit, or someone folding a T-shirt in a perfect square with a single swift motion. Some of the best posts are about sharing our sense of wonder, and Web curios are often captivating. They're the grown-up version of "Watch me pull this quarter from behind my ear."

I favor stories about weird places:

> In Texas, twenty miles southwest of Abilene, is an old missile silo that's become an attraction for divers. The once top-secret underground bunker used to contain nuclear weapons, but the concrete silo now contains a quiet well of groundwater. Divers enter the complex by descending a long staircase, passing through several blast doors and the launch control bunker, and entering a tunnel that leads them to the silo. From there they enter the deep pool of water, which is fifty-two feet wide. A pile of metal debris and the missile control station wait below, eighteen stories underwater.

2

Thirty Minutes Away from the TV

Skip the sitcom rerun, and open up a blank screen. With half an hour, you have enough time to produce a post that will leave you feeling smug.

21 | Address the public.

Revive the lost art of letter writing by addressing fellow citizens. Here's my open letter to Boston:

> Dear Boston,
>
> Why are you walking so close to me? It's just you, and me, and this vast stretch of lonely sidewalk that empties into the horizon. I have my dance space, you have your dance space, and yet you're always all up in my dance space, Boston. What it is with you? You are walking faster than me, it's true, but there's plenty of room for you to pass me. Six feet or more in which to pass. The width of a small football field in which to pass.
>
> And yet, here you are again, half a foot behind me. I cannot see you, though I can feel your hot breath on the back of my neck. Common sense tells me that no one walks this close, in my blind spot, on a virtually empty sidewalk, unless he or she is about to take my purse. But when I stop and turn to the side, forcing you to pass, it startles you. It turns out you were just plodding along, innocently, mere inches from my spine.
>
> I know you don't mean any harm, and you seem like such a nice city, and you obviously have no designs on my purse, but please stop it. You're creeping me out.
>
> Sincerely,
> Maggie

22 | Play their games.

Pitching in on a community project is the Web version of going outside to play. Though the couch is cushy and warm, and the chips within easy reach, we all have to get out sometime. Metaphorically speaking, of course. Let's not be rash.

Look for a community project that interests you, and bring something to the party. Your contribution can be as small as posting a response on Ask Metafilter (http://ask.metafilter.com), a community site where users pose questions and wait for answers. If you'd like to do some heavier lifting, there are tons of projects that require more time. Post Secret (http://postsecret.blogspot.com) asks readers to send in secrets on handmade postcards, and posts a few each week.

Do your part, and then point readers to your contribution. Perhaps you'll inspire them to make something worthwhile as well.

23 | Define your inscrutables.

Is nothing sacred? Well, not really. You're the type who puts it all out there—relationship details, depression-med doses, dark family secrets. With all that online information waiting to be discovered by your stunned parents, you might be surprised at how much readers still don't know about you.

They wouldn't recognize your handwriting on a note, be able to discern your laughter in a group, or even know how tall you are. Take a photo of your handwriting, show readers your wardrobe, or record a short clip of yourself humming a tune. You've covered the big topics, now get to the details. Here's a sample of my handwriting for the record:

Famous among dozens.

HOORAY FOR STUFF!

24 | Make it easy.

Coping mechanisms help us pretend that the day is long enough to fit everything in. Tell us about the small habits you've adopted to make your life run more smoothly. You automated bill payments, stopped sorting your socks and silverware before putting them in the drawers, or maybe you cook all day Sunday to make meals you can freeze for the week.

Life Hacker (www.lifehacker.com) is devoted to productivity tips. They offer great packing advice:

> The Universal Packing List (http://upl.codeq.info/index.jsp) is a terrific online application that allows you to build a customized packing list, complete with reminders and tips, for any traveling you'll be doing....
>
> It works by having you fill out an online form with details about your trip, and some details about the kind of list you're looking for. Then, based on your answers, it gives you a customized list of what to pack as well as some general advice and reminders. It's very simple, yet very effective.

25 | Offer classified information.

Free time, untold riches, a perfect Friday night date—your life is missing all kinds of good stuff. Have you considered advertising? Write up a brief classified ad, the kind people used to run when they had to pay by the word, seeking something you could use.

You can also reverse the process by offering to sell something you'd be glad to give up. Christmas with the relatives? Haul it away. Awkward conversation with my co-worker about his lack of personal hygiene: going cheap!

Or try a missed connection ad:

> Corner of Albuquerque and Main, you were driving a Porsche, and I was waiting for the bus. Our eyes met. It felt like destiny. Is it me, or are you the life I was supposed to have?

26 | Share your expertise.

You have a foolproof hangover cure, and you're keeping it from the world? Do you know what that's doing to your karma? Tell the people, before you lose an eye or something.

Whatever you know how to do, teach the masses your secret. It could be something small, like how to skip stones, hang a spoon from the end of your nose, or make a spicy cup of ginger tea. Whatever it is, you can educate your readers.

Merlin Mann's (www.43Folders.com) hacks for Moleskine-brand notebooks are legendary:

> Spine Icons—I know some of you, like me, are multiple-Moleskine nerds. It's sad, but this is how God's made us. So, this means you might have a lined notebook, a sketch book, a music notebook, or even a storyboard notebook—all of the same size and outward appearance. Using a silver Sharpie or the like, make a small icon or letter at the same place on each spine to remind you which is which.

27 | Show some love.

If you think your Netflix queue or your TiVo lineup says a lot about you, consider your friends.

Chilling, isn't it?

Jokes aside, the people around you are doing worthy things—raising healthy kids, perfecting a signature mixed drink, making a fresh start. Write little profiles of your friends, counting up the reasons you respect them or the times they've surprised or impressed you.

You can interview them, or just write up a paragraph or two. Tell us who your friends are, and why you picked them to be part of your life.

28 | Blow your budget.

Imagine you've just come into ten million dollars. How do you spend it? Put together a wish list of epic proportions—perhaps a six-burner gas grill (for your yacht). You can go real estate shopping, or plan where you'd stop on a trip around the world. You can right a wrong, or start a foundation in your name.

If you're feeling whimsical, find out exactly how much it would cost to fill a pool with ping pong balls or rent the Brooklyn Bridge for a block party. If ten million isn't enough, increase your windfall until your rock-and-roll lifestyle is within reach.

29 | Place yourself.

Platial (www.platial.com) is a Google Maps mashup that lets you create maps with any context you like. You can make maps of the bookstores you adore, the places where you've made out, the bookstores where you've made out, and so on. You can also join forces with community members to map your collective consciousness.

Together, you can build maps of where to get wireless access, where to find the best hot chocolate in New York, or where you can go to ride a carousel anywhere in the United States. Start simple with a map that tells readers where you've traveled in the world. You can easily create a group map in Platial and encourage other users to join in.

A user named Paiges created the Hopeless Romantic group map (www.platial.com/paiges/map/1535), with this description:

> Lost love. Missed chances. Unrequited love. Never meant to last. Doomed from the start. Wishing I had the nerve. Still thinking of you. Never forget you. I left this for you. I want you to know. My Heart still aches for you. I thought it mattered.

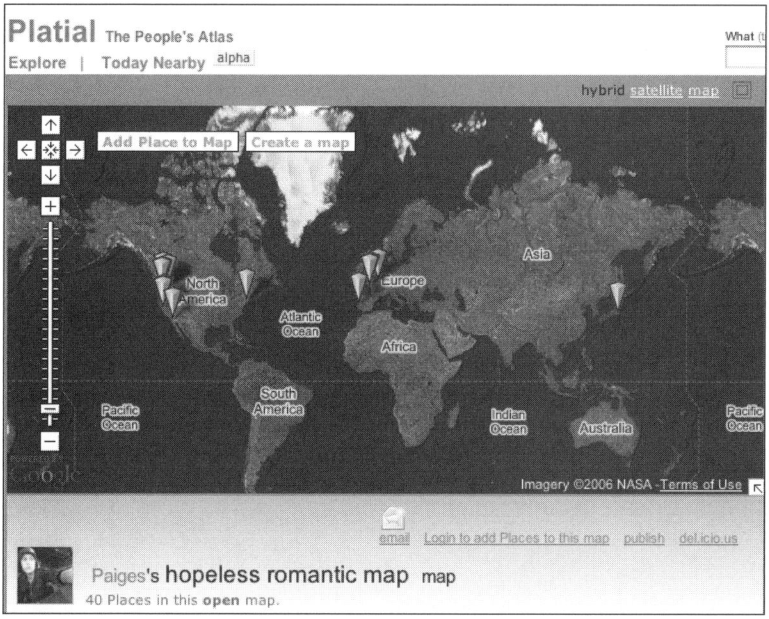

Or just tell us where to find a good beer.

30 | Be yourself.

> Things I Like: music, dogs, reading, movies, hanging out with friends...

Honey, who doesn't? As long as you're writing one of those ubiquitous *lists de likes*, at least make it worth reading. Your readers don't care whether you love kittens, they care about the quirky things you love, the things *only* you love. Say something surprising.

Brittney Gilbert (http://brittney.typepad.com) writes:

> When I cook eggs I can't just toss the shell without first crushing it in my palm. I like the prickly sensation of the broken, jagged shell in my skin.

Now you have our attention.

31 | Dig in.

What makes your mouth water? A thick milkshake and salty fries on the boardwalk, or prime rib and bourbon crème brûlée over a linen napkin—tell us about your perfect meal.

It can be one you've already eaten, a meal you like to prepare, or one you've yet to enjoy. If it's something you make yourself, supply recipes and photos to accompany your post. Or maybe your perfect meal has more to do with the environment and the company than the actual food. Explain whom you'd invite, where you'd land, and whether you'd choose breakfast, lunch, or dinner.

32 | Break it off.

He mentions that he was on his high school track team—a dozen times. She won't shut up about her dad. He keeps a photo of his ex in his wallet. She's, well, a little bit married.

What are your relationship deal breakers? Some folks are annoyed if a date shows up ten minutes late. Others look for something weightier, like a felony record. Have you ever rejected someone over something that seems insignificant to your friends? Or do you have selective blindness for red flags?

33 | Spread the words.

Between subscriptions to *The New Yorker, The Week, Harper's,* and so on, you haven't read a book in three years. You trip over a copy of *Offshore Engineer* on the way to bathroom. Your cat is sleeping on the back issues of *Packaging Digest.*

Save us from your fate by making a digest version of the articles you've perused recently. Pull great paragraphs, point out absurdities, or just tell us about the stories that changed your perspective.

This is my collection of excellent headlines from back issues of *Martha Stewart Living:*

- Putting Baking Stones to Use
- Painting a Window
- Why Scald Milk?
- Ironing Ruffles and Pleats
- Arrangement of the Month: Forsythia Fan
- The Finest Seasalt
- Ruffles: They are much more than a dressmaker's detail
- Organizing Pots and Pans
- Ironing a Table Cloth
- Pantries of Maine

34 | Give a tour.

You have twenty-four hours in San Francisco, and you cannot get back on a plane until you've had a San Francisco burrito. This burrito must have a grilled tortilla (as opposed to steamed), evenly distributed ingredients, and flavorful, gristle-free meat. Where will you find such a specimen? Well, follow my blog link to Burrito Eater (www.burritoeater.com), where the site proprietor is working his way through the approximately 170 taquerias in town.

I have hundreds of other bits of advice about San Francisco, and you know just as much about your own town. Take advantage of your insider status, and give us a tour. If you live in a small town, tell us the best place to squish pennies on the tracks, or which day the pies are made fresh at the café. Point us to the astounding array of driveway stains at your Uncle Mitch's place. We'd like to know more about where you live.

35 | Show some skin.

How did you get those scars? The one on your thumb is from when you were three and you wondered whether scissors could cut skin. The one on your stomach is from your emergency appendectomy. Your boss figured you had to be in the hospital, because it was the only reason you'd ever be late to work without calling.

Your scars indicate what type of life you've lived. Whether you're athletic, fighting for your health, or just occasionally clumsy, let each scar remind you of the story behind it.

Blogjam offers a "Name My Scars" (www.blogjam.com/name_my_scars) feature:

> I recently had a knee operation, and am now gruesomely scarred for life. As I have to live with these mementos for the rest of my days, I thought it would be nice if I could give the pair some personality, something to make me feel more at home with the disfigurement. You can help me out by suggesting names for the scars—they can be traditional boys or girls names, but feel free to be as adventurous as you like.

36 | Swallow your pride.

Did your pack-a-day habit begin on a patch of scrub grass behind the gym? Are you concerned that your hipster friends will find out you were once a cheerleader? Maybe all of your high school and junior high memories are coiled in a tight little ball at the back of your brain. Well, it's time to drag them out, mewling and squinting against the sunlight.

Scan in photos of you in uniform with an awkward haircut, offer up the choicest yearbook inscriptions, or tell us about your top-three suspensions. The more miserable you were, the more endearing you'll become. Here's a spectacular photo of me from 1993, would that you could see the fruity colors in my rainbow shirt.

37 | Find the objects of your affection.

At 3 a.m., the fire alarm wakes you. You realize that the house is aflame, and that you're sleeping naked. After grabbing a robe, and making sure that people and pets are out of the building, what would you search for next?

Say you reach for practical things—your hard drive, your passport. Maybe you run for the family photos, the cross-stitch your niece made, or your first guitar. Do you have a suitcase you've meticulously packed for emergencies? If so, have you talked to someone about that?

38 | Start here.

Millions of people think they'll write a book one day. Of those millions, ten people have actually decided on a book title, and maybe fifteen have written the first sentence.

If you want to write a book, really and truly, you'll need to spend some time filling in the blank space on a page or a screen. Fortunately, the input box for your blog is bite-sized. It only wants a paragraph or so. Surely you can manage that.

You can set up a separate serial-novel blog in a few minutes, or mix in book excerpts with your regular posts. Start with a few sentences a day, or try to hit 500 words, whatever you can do consistently.

If slow plodding doesn't appeal, wait until November and join the fray of National Novel Writing Month (www.nanowrimo.org):

> Because of the limited writing window, the only thing that matters in NaNoWriMo is output. It's all about quantity, not quality. The kamikaze approach forces you to lower your expectations, take risks, and write on the fly.

39 | Choose your words.

So, you want to throw something at my head when I suggest writing a novel. I have no idea how hectic your life is! You barely have time to take a shower!

OK, if you're taking finals, or you have a newborn, or you've just purchased the *Buffy the Vampire Slayer* DVD collection, you may need to reign things in a bit.

Instead of committing to your masterpiece, try writing the shortest story imaginable. Give yourself a hundred words to tell a complete narrative. It's more difficult than you'd expect, but you'll still have time to nap afterward. An example from Mighty Girl (www.mightygirl.com):

> This man is standing barefoot in the gutter of a busy street wearing his white terrycloth bathrobe. He has not come out to retrieve the paper, or turn off the sprinklers, or check his mail. He's come out to enjoy this fine Thanksgiving Day and watch the cars go by. He spits, takes a drag of his cigarette, and sighs contentedly.

40 | Cower before us.

Sometimes, rats swim up sewer lines and paddle around in your toilet, waiting for you to make a midnight visit. Occasionally, something sinister lurks under your bed hoping to grab your ankles before you climb in. (The same thing waits under your car when you leave it in parking garages at night.) A swim in the lake on a balmy afternoon can go from zero to Stephen King with the appearance of an innocuous blob of oil—a blob that turns out to be carnivorous. I mean, you never know.

All kinds of scary things happen, just not as often as we anticipate them. What are your irrational fears, and where did they come from?

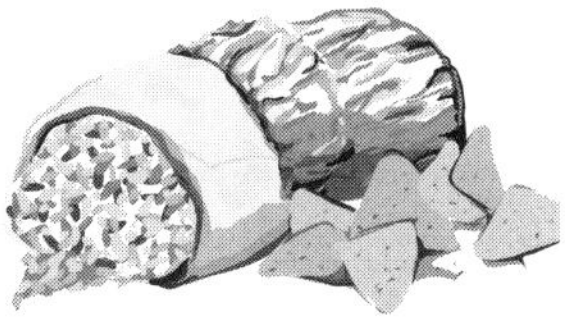

3

An Hour at the Screen

Here you are with time to spare. An entire hour stretches before you—you don't need a nap, no one wants anything from you. Want to make something cool? Dig in.

41 | Show some family pride.

It seems like we mostly pay tribute to people only at their funerals, which is kind of horrifying when you think about it. If you're searching for a gift for the relative who has everything, give your words. A well-timed tribute to a loved one makes birthdays, anniversaries, or congratulations more meaningful.

Every month, Heather B. Armstrong (www.dooce.com) posts a letter for her baby girl, Leta. She sums up what's happened that month, and tells Leta how she's changing:

> Sometimes your constant mimicry of us is a little maddening. If you are acting grumpy and we ask you what is wrong you answer, "Wrong." If I point to your father and ask, "Who is that?" you answer, "That." If we want you to say please before we give you something I'll ask you, "What do you say?" and you'll answer, "Say." This is more funny than it is frustrating, I have to admit, and it has brought some of our own habits into stark relief. A few weeks ago I was getting dressed for the day and I walked into the bedroom wearing nothing but my underwear. You and your father were sitting on the bed reading books, and when you saw me walk through the door you assessed what I was wearing and then let out a guttural imitation of a construction worker: "HeeeeeEEEEEEEEYYYYYY! YeaaaaaaHHHHHHH!" Your father laughed and then admitted, "I couldn't have said it better myself."

42 | Make your timeline.

- Age 6: You are terrified that you will wake to find yourself atop a Ferris wheel.
- Age 10: Having defeated your arch-nemesis, you are the reigning tetherball champion of the schoolyard.
- Age 15: None of the people you thought you liked have turned out to be very likable.
- Age 20: You are dating badly.
- Age 24: You are still dating badly.

Make a personal timeline of your past. Describe what was happening at each stage of your life, and how those memories fit together. You can make a forthright list of major events, or talk about how you were feeling and what mattered to you at a particular age.

43 | Show us a good time.

How is it that your parties inspire spontaneous food fights, table dancing, and spectacular (but unfortunate) hookups that live in infamy? Perhaps it's the unlimited tequila.

Some of us have trouble pulling brunch together, while others can convince guests to don lampshades and conga through the apartment building. If you're one of the latter, give the masses some of your magic dust. Tell us about a recent party plan, outlining the number of guests, the type of food, how much prep time we'll need. Tell us how you get your guests to loosen up—serving your signature cocktails in extra-large glasses, for example.

44 | Take inventory.

What do you collect? Photograph each item and explain where you got it and why (or whether) you love it.

Bill Keaggy is working on a book compiling his grocery list collection (www.grocerylists.org). He has over 1,000 found lists; one of my favorites is the classic PMS grocery list:

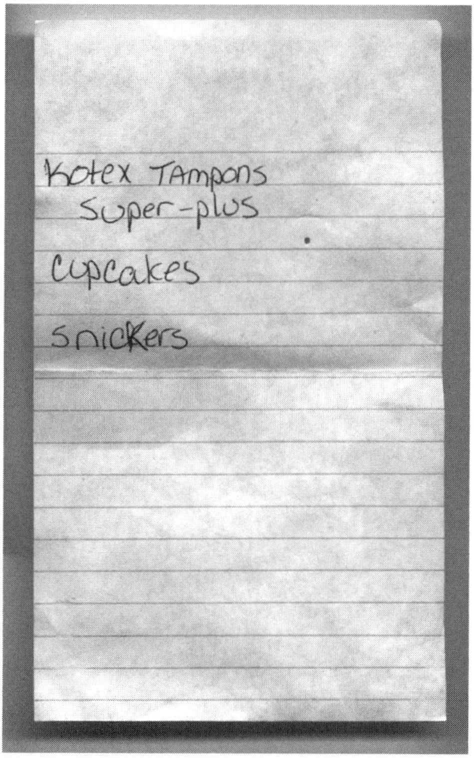

45 | Ante up.

You're a good person: you feel bad when you hurt someone's feelings; you try not to laugh at people who aren't as smart as you; you're fond of puppies. You may only have a tiny bit of power, but you want to use it for good. And that's a noble endeavor, my friend.

Do some research and point your readers to a few worthy charities. While you're at it, explain what their donations would accomplish for the organizations you list. Then put your feet up and bask in the warm glow of self-satisfaction.

46 | Review your résumé.

Your job pays your bills, defines your life, or something in between. Whether you organize the office hula-hoop contest or cringe when someone calls you to the break room for lard-frosted birthday cake, tell us your work stories.

Do you remember the outfit you wore to your first interview? Have you ever been fired? When did you first realize that your boss would have trouble sharpening a pencil without help? Or maybe your boss was a mentor who changed the way you thought about your job.

Anil Dash (www.dashes.com/anil) works for Six Apart, a company that makes blogging tools. Here's what he says about his job:

> I spend a lot of time doing public speaking. So far I've managed to create a PowerPoint presentation featuring Dr. Phil, a pair of handcuffs, an American flag, a cliché kitty, the Enron logo, the phrase "OMG WTF" in 72-point font, a line graph in which both the X and Y axes are completely unlabeled, the Easter bunny, and Santa Claus. It should be pretty easy to work in a game of Assassin. I love my job.

47 | Promote truth.

You already know the basics:

- Don't fill up on bread.
- Wear sunscreen.
- If you're putting an air freshener in the bathroom, don't choose one that smells like food.

You're a font of wisdom, and you're getting sharper every year. Outline ten truths you believe to be universal. You can tell us how you came to your conclusions, or explain how your beliefs have changed over the years. If you're feeling ambitious, check back on this list in a few years to see if you still agree with yourself.

48 | Hang your head.

For some, an ill-chosen phrase is enough to get them blushing. *You*, on the other hand, could run into your grandmother while you're buying a pack of condoms without losing your composure. The cringe-worthiness of a situation depends greatly on your temperament.

Outline your gravest humiliation—you were flirting and spilled your drink dramatically, you froze in front of the microphone, you sat in something unpleasant and no one told you until after the graduation ceremony. Whatever it is, we feel your pain. After we spend a few minutes pointing and laughing, that is.

49 | Engage in finger pointing, snickering.

Hypocrisy, religious fanaticism, actors recording "break-out" CDs. There's so much out there to mock. Try your hand at satire by spoofing something. Make fun of an ad, a web page, or a social phenomenon.

Matthew Haughey recently poked fun at the motion-detecting MacSaber application by performing a tribute to the Star Wars Kid (www.jedimaster.net). Instead of using a quarterstaff as a faux light saber, Matthew used his new laptop. By tying in Star Wars, a new Mac application, and a well-known Web meme, Matthew hit the golden trifecta of total geek-out. The result is hilarious (http://a.wholelottanothing.org/2006/05/macbook_man.html). You can blog your own videos by signing on with You Tube (www.youtube.com) and linking out to videos that you've stashed there.

00:03 / 00:12
Size:

00:07 / 00:12
Size:

00:09 / 00:12
Size:

50 | Clean house.

Some things we hold on to way past their expiration date: the rocks you collected from who knows where, the bubble bath that's "too good to use," the dream of becoming a rock star. Time to empty your closets and fill up your blog by posting about the things you need to let go.

Eden Marriott Kennedy (www.fussy.org) wrote that carrying some of her old stuff to her new home would be like "strapping a bunch of tombstones to my back." Instead, she photographed the items and told their stories before donating them to charity.

Here's her story about a sweater that used to belong to her friend Tamara's father, Skip:

> I could write 2,000 words on Skip alone.... Sometimes when I spent the night we'd wake up to Skip playing bongos in the basement and singing along with Stevie Wonder records. Skip wore love beads.... He had a blurry little tattoo of St. Anthony's crutch on his shoulder, and after he died Tamara told me he'd always wanted to turn it into an apple tree. When I heard that, I realized that was the tattoo I wanted to get (as some of you know, my first name is Eden). I got an apple tree tattooed on my shoulder and when I went to Tamara's wedding I showed it to her mom and she kind of laughed and cried at the same time.

51 | Risk everything.

You can live your whole life following the path of least resistance. No risks, no unknowns, no discomfort. And goodness knows that we all dream of a tombstone that reads, "I was comfortable."

Tell us about the biggest risk you could take in your life right now. It doesn't have to be cliff-diving dramatic. Perhaps it would be easier to jump out of a plane than to go after your dream job. Or maybe something that seems simple to other people is terrifying to you. What would you risk if you had the nerve?

52 | Wear it well.

So. What are you wearing?

C'mon, you can tell us. We all have a favorite outfit or two—pants that make our bums look great, a shirt we reach for when we know the ex will be at the party. Open your closet and show us what's inside.

Describe your perfect interview outfit, the fashion disasters that have haunted you, the items you've bought and never worn (or will never wear again). Or just use your clothes to remind you of where you were and what you were doing when you last wore them.

53 | Categorize your readers.

It can be so satisfying to test people, and then put them into neat little categories. Try your hand at writing a quiz. Quizbox (www.quizbox.com/builder) can help with the structure and will tally your points for you, helping you create a quiz to host on your own blog.

Evany Thomas (www.evany.com) recently wrote a book called *The Secret Language of Sleep*, and she posted a companion quiz on her blog to help couples identify their ideal sleeping positions (www.evany.com/sleeptest).

¡Dormimos! is the pose of two highly unique opposites: the Social Butterfly and the Homebody. To outsiders, the combination may seem ill advised. "Why doesn't she find someone who will keep her company at these wine sips?" people wonder. Yet every butterfly periodically needs a place to rest and recuperate, and that's exactly what the corresponding half of ¡Dormimos! provides: a stationary flower for the butterfly to cling to.

Illustration by Amelia Bauer

54 | Get defensive.

Spray cheese is a delicacy. People really underestimate Keanu Reeves. Bikini waxing doesn't even hurt. Wal-Mart is a perfect model of how a healthy business should function in a capitalist society. Airplane food is super good. You have to be totally talented to be a mime—like, a good one anyway. Most commercials are designed to be entertaining. Starbucks makes a good latte. The thing about diets is, they really teach you self-discipline. Traffic jams are fine if you have a book on tape or something.

What do you love that no one else loves? Defend the indefensible.

55 | Take sides.

The conversation turns to a big topic—the death sentence, human rights, censorship, religious freedom—and you turn your nose into an empty drink, swishing the ice cubes around. Perhaps you're not sure what to say because you don't know enough about those things to make an educated decision. Maybe you don't consider yourself a political person, or you try not to worry about things you don't feel you can change.

Have you ever wondered, though, what your opinion would be if you knew more? Take an hour or so to gather facts about a particular issue. Do a little balanced research and figure out how you really feel. If politics doesn't appeal, try researching things that do apply to your everyday life. What are the major schools of thought on child rearing, for example, or could you be buying products from companies whose activities you find immoral?

Link to the research you use, and tell readers your conclusions. Then, let them draw their own.

56 | Go places.

Have you had tea in the shadow of the Taj Mahal, or do you just head out to the front porch for your morning cup? Think of the places that have meaning in your life and write about the memories they evoke.

Where have you been, and what did you take away? You can choose homes you've lived in over the years, schools you've attended, or countries you've visited. Did you have a special hiding place when you were a kid? What places did you frequent in your hometown? Describe the general feelings they evoke and why.

57 | Say thanks.

The last time you wrote a thank you note, it was after your mom sat you down at a table with stickers, colored pens, and instructions to thank Aunt Ginny for the lovely sweater. You're no ingrate, but perhaps you have been a tad ungrateful over the years. Now you have some catching up to do.

There's someone out there who deserves your thanks. Maybe it's a stranger who helped you gather the contents of the bag you spilled, or a friend who taught you to stop saying nasty things about yourself. Post a thank you note to someone who made your life a little nicer.

58 | Think back.

Tell us what you were doing during the major historical events of your lifetime. Here's a brief timeline of U.S. history to jog your memory:

- President Kennedy assassinated
- The Beatles appear on *The Ed Sullivan Show*
- Martin Luther King, Jr. assassinated
- Robert Kennedy assassinated
- Man walks on the moon
- President Nixon resigns
- President Reagan shot
- Challenger explodes
- Berlin Wall falls

- Persian Gulf war
- Rodney King riots
- Waco, Texas standoff
- Oklahoma City bombing
- Presidential election recount
- 9/11 attacks
- Iraq war
- Columbia explodes
- Hurricane Katrina
- Dick Cheney accidentally shoots his friend in the face

What were your thoughts when you first heard the news?

59 | Offer survival tips.

It started with a few passive aggressive notes—on the bathroom mirror, then in the fridge, and then on the computer. Things escalated to open arguments about how to split the toilet paper bill by "percentage of use," and weekly email reports on how inconsiderate you were.

You finally moved out when the phone was disconnected because the bill was months overdue, even though you'd been dutifully contributing your share. Tell your quirky, disturbing, and certifiably insane roommate stories, and then find yourself a cheap studio apartment.

60 | Ask science.

Answer an inane question that keeps you awake at night by conducting an utterly unnecessary experiment. Can you get a mile of ink out of a single pen? Which method of shoelace tying leads to longer lace life?

Michael Buffington challenged a friend to swallow an entire tablespoon of ground cinnamon, and then recorded the results (www.michaelbuffington.com/cc2k1).

Rob Cockerham (www.cockeyed.com) has a section of his site—called "How Much Is Inside?"—wherein he finds innovative ways to measure the contents of various household items. Turns out that one roll of Glad Wrap can wrap 220 Rice Krispy treats, a box of Cheerios on a string measures about 73 feet, and one tube of MAC lipstick can (and did) cover his friend's feet and legs just about up to her knees. Anyone else want to buy a drink for Rob?

4

Take Your Time

Have a glass of lemonade, put your feet up, and flip through this chapter in a leisurely manner. These projects will take a while, but where do you have to be? You've got all the time in the world.

61 | Collect the greatest hits.

So your blog gets Slashdotted one day when you're in bed sleeping off the flu. You're barely staying hydrated, let alone keeping up with your site. A few days later, you realize that, when your traffic spiked by 20,000 readers, your top post was a two-sentence throwaway about the awesome sneakers you just scored. (On sale!)

Crap.

Traffic, and life, are unpredictable, so once you've built a healthy selection of posts, pull the best ones aside and put them where visitors can find them easily. You'll give loyal readers a place to go on days when you're off your game, and you'll improve the odds of converting new readers into regular visitors.

A few of Matthew Baldwin's (www.defectiveyeti.com) favorite posts:

> PRACTICE WHAT YOU PERK
>
> "My barista is jittery and high-strung. I find this comforting, like a barber with well-coifed hair."
>
> DEARTH OF MIRTH
>
> "Saw a headline today: 'Botox Injections Popular For Erasing Laugh Lines.' Yes sir, there's nothing sexier than a woman who looks as if she hasn't smiled a day in her life."

62 | Hit the stacks.

Bibliophiles, prepare to forfeit your spare time. Library Thing (www.librarything.com) is an online tool that lets you catalog and categorize your books. You can create a "virtual shelf" with the covers of books you've been reading, or make a list with tags and information about how other users relate to a particular book.

The Zeitgeist section shows you how books are behaving across the site, with lists of top authors and books, most reviewed books, and more. You'll see users who own the same books as you and find out what they recommend. You can, of course, opt to display your collection on your blog.

63 | Make contact.

You miss real mail. The kind with a stamp placed on the corner of the envelope and your address scrawled out in human handwriting. Get a P.O. box and turn your readers into pen pals. You can send postcards, bookmarks, photos, and small tokens of affection. Agree on themes for swaps and post photos of the results on your blog.

In Judith Zissman's 20 Things Project (www.20things.org), she asked twenty participants to send her twenty small pieces of art within twenty days. She then prepared packages so that each person would receive a piece of artwork from one of the other participants. A few samples:

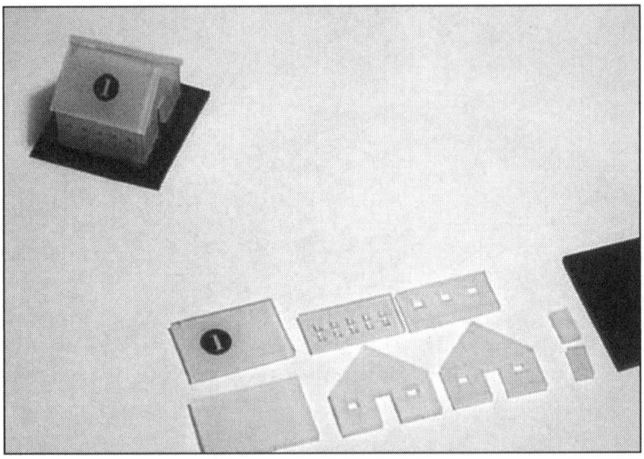

"Shrinky Dink Houses" by Rick Mullarky

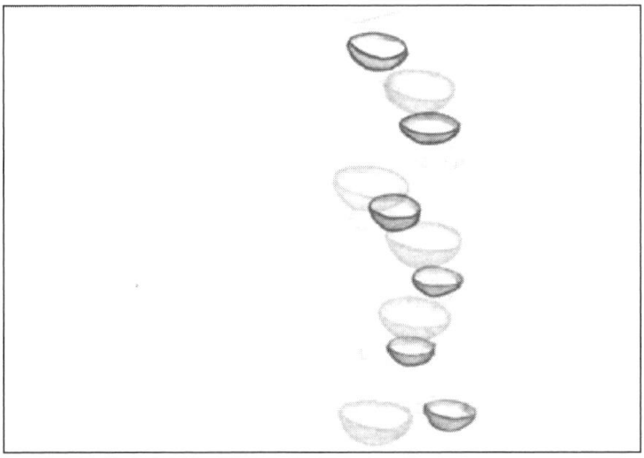

"Tornado" by Sasha Wizansky

"Worth(less)" by Rena Tom

64 | Get dibs.

I'd like to collect decaying mansions and move them all to one neighborhood so I can repaint them and plant trees in the front yards. Unfortunately, I don't have a few million laying around for my mansion collection just yet, so I'll have to settle for perusing real estate ads and whimpering.

Start your own virtual collection of items that are too unwieldy or expensive to collect in real life. Whatever your passion—airplanes, modern art, pricey jewelry—pick twenty pieces for your online collection and rotate them out as the mood strikes you.

65 | Rope friends in.

You have a vision: a plate of nachos so large that it eclipses the dining room table. This is a brilliant idea. But cheese is expensive and it takes forever to grate, and how will you fit it all in the oven? You'll need a team—Team Nacho.

Grand ideas are bloggable ideas, but you may need a little help from your friends to make them possible. Blowing bubbles off the town bridge is a lot cooler if a hundred people do it. Find a group of creative types and ban together to record your wackiness for our vicarious pleasure.

Of course, you can do this on a much smaller scale—finding an illustrator for a comic strip you'd like to write, for example. But wouldn't a hundred people blowing bubbles off a bridge be cool? It totally would.

66 | Keep track.

Lots of bloggers use the space in their sidebar to keep a running list. While the sidebar is well suited for small posts (like brief links) that would otherwise get lost amid longer entries, it's even better for building an article one snip at a time. Think of it as a text collage. The parts aren't worth much, but they add up to make something more intriguing.

One at a time, list things you need to remember: books to read, products to buy, recipes to try. Or you can take a less concrete approach: moments that make you happy throughout your day, things that need to change, things you've tried for the first time.

Once your list has enough material, move it to a permanent home and start a new one.

67 | Tell us what you've done.

Give us a day in your life. Record everything you did in a typical day or week. What you spent, where you went, be as detailed as you like. Do the results bore you? Time to take up knife throwing, my friend.

My cousin, Matthew (www.childsplayx2.com), recently recorded a day in his life as the suspiciously competent father of twins. Here's the first hour of his typical day:

> 6 A.M.—Wake-up time. If I'm lucky, JT and/or Bri will not have awakened during the night. It's really a toss-up whether they will wake up or not. If they are sick (which covers about 80 percent of the past five months) then you can be sure one will wake up. If they have not awakened, I go get them out of bed at 6:05 a.m. while Andrea showers. I have already laid out their clothes and diapers. If fortune is on my side, I can usually scoop one out of their crib before the other knows I'm there. I then change diapers and clothing in our bedroom and put whichever baby I have on the floor to play while I go get the other one. Hopefully the one on the floor will play quietly but if he/she is hungry, I have to hurry to get the other one ready while listening to wailing.

Are you wondering why the poor guy bothered to type this up instead of taking a nap? Me too.

68 | Let us cheer you on.

You're digging your way out of a mess, and we'd like to root for you. Use your blog to find others who are running the same gauntlet, and inspire them to take action.

David Beach created Die Old (www.dieold.org) to help him track his weight loss and to encourage others to choose healthier lives. He writes about his struggles and successes along the way. So far he's lost twenty-five pounds! He writes:

> I've often wondered if people would treat me differently if I were of normal size. Would they somehow take me more seriously or would there be an unspoken additional respect because I was fit that would translate to more opportunities for me? Sometimes I get the feeling that this [is] true. Do fit people have an advantage just because of their appearance? Certainly this seems to be the case with women. I know it's not politically correct to point it out, but I think many women would agree. It's subtle, but it's there. I guess it's a form of discrimination. It may not be true at all, it could be just my own insecurity about how I think I look fogging reality.

69 | Send a message.

You have 15,000 emails saved on your hard drive. There's got to be some good material in there. Mine your old files and post amusing excerpts from emails of yore. Here's one of my email moments from Mighty Girl:

> SUBJECT: A college friend reminisces about his youth.
>
> EXCERPT: My mother would frequently record tape cassettes and send them to my grandparents, uncles and aunts, et al. to mark our progress (this was before the invention of the motion-picture camera). On one of these tapes, my mother tells me, "Stop that," seventy-eight times in a matter of fifteen minutes. One of my favorite lines is when she yells, "You better NOT pee on the couch."

70 | Put it aside.

Thirty years from now, your children will look back and be dumbfounded by the size of your current cell phone. Make an online time capsule for your blog.

Include everyday items alongside historical markers. You can post newspaper articles of current events next to photos of your car and your house. Note how much a few things cost, like gasoline or a loaf of bread. Share your ticket stubs, and mention the pop culture that has your attention. Finally, consider including a letter to yourself that you can return to read in a decade or so. After you've posted everything, burn the files to a CD for good measure.

71 | Become an expert.

You love to cook, so you buy the cookbooks recommended by your Food Network heroes and start working through them. About a year later, you've begun to visit a butcher shop, a bakery, a produce stand, and a cheese shop to obtain the ingredients for one meal. Soon thereafter, you start saying moderately annoying things like, "It doesn't even count as chocolate if it isn't at least 80 percent cacao." Look who's becoming an expert.

You have an interest that could turn into a passion if you just gave it a little room to breathe. Start pulling together links, studying up, and connecting the dots to see if you can turn your blog into the go-to resource for people who share your passion.

72 | Do the right thing.

Choose a cause that makes you want to fight, and tell your readers what you plan to do—save a historic building from demolition, give someone job skills, send a kid to school.

If you make your aim concrete, you'll find it easier to enlist support. People can grasp the kind of effort it will take to raise $500 for a scholarship; they're less inclined to pitch in for something more overwhelming, like ending illiteracy.

Lay out a game plan, and keep everyone informed as you work to reach your goal. Words have so much power. Use yours to make things better.

73 | Collect people.

Interview someone you admire but don't necessarily know. Contact authors, local personalities, or interesting people you've encountered.

Leah Peterson (www.leahpeah.com/blog) started talking to her favorite bloggers a few years ago, and now has dozens of blogger interviews posted on her site. Here's an excerpt from an interview with Melissa Summers (www.suburbanbliss.net):

> *Worst/best experience regarding something you wrote in your blog or put out on the net?*
>
> I made fun of a family member's new baby's name. It was when my site was just 5 months old and I had 50 readers. I didn't think they'd ever see it, but they did (as people ALWAYS will. They ALWAYS will. Always.). I find it hard to believe they didn't know their son's name would get them some ribbing but I would never, ever make fun of someone's child's name to their face and therefore I should never have done it on the internet. Lesson learned.
>
> *Astounding facts about you:*
>
> In the third grade I designed a Girl Scout patch for our region's big camping event. All the campers from Southeastern Michigan voted on which should be manufactured and mine was picked.
>
> Guess where it is now? No, really guess, because I have no idea and would like to find it.

74 | Present your memories.

Instead of making a scrapbook of an important set of memories, make a live version on your blog. Meg Pearson and Rahul Young recently finished a year-long trip around the world, which they recorded online at their blog, Take Me to the Volcano (http://tothevolcano.blogspot.com). They included an itinerary and photos, and posted about the experiences they had on the road.

> After an 11-hour bus ride (it was supposed to take 6), and a 6-hour ferry ride (it was supposed to take 3), we made it to Zanzibar! Found a cheap place to stay, took a much-needed shower, headed out to the street food stalls on the ocean, and paid $.20 for a big glass of fresh sugarcane lime juice while feasting on barbequed tuna skewers and roasted cassava. It's good here. It's really good here.

75 | Be neighborly.

Start a blog or a regular feature of stories about living in your neighborhood or town. If you'd like, you can even let the neighbors post. From 1998 to 2002, Derek Powazek maintained San Francisco Stories (www.sfstories.com), allowing readers to post their own anecdotes. He categorized the stories by neighborhood. Here, Derek shares a few secrets about his neighborhood, Cole Valley:

- Dryer number 39 at Doug's Suds will give you 10 minutes per quarter, instead of the standard 7. Washer 12 used to count tapping on the coin slot as quarters, but Doug fixed it.
- Don't ever lie in the grass at the park where the N-Judah comes out of the Sunset Tunnel. As a dog walker, trust me on this one.
- The flyer that was up in mid-June about a dog found on the roof of a garage? That was Buddy. He's fine now.
- The French bakery that opened recently is actually neither French nor a bakery. The croissants are cooked by Mexicans across town and delivered every morning.

76 | Change everything.

Perhaps you're planning a big life change, like a new career, a wedding, a baby, or something equally dramatic. Tell us about your intentions, and take us along on your journey.

Ariel Meadow Stallings (www.electrolicious.com) got married in 2004 and gave readers all the details about the wedding. It was so much fun that Ariel is now writing a book called *Offbeat Bride*, which chronicles her experiences and offers tips for unique weddings. An excerpt from her site:

> Andreas has been trying to find just the right shirt to wear for the wedding. Something sort of flamenco, sort of Don Juan de Marco. "Like a pirate shirt?" I kept asking. No, no, he said. Not a pirate shirt.
>
> Today he found the shirt he wants. What's it called? Spice Pirate Shirt. Even better? It's from International Male!
>
> Sometimes our wedding is so freaky that even I don't know what to say.

77 | Show us your B-side.

Why do you always choke up when you hear Corey Hart's "Sunglasses at Night"? You're kind of scaring us.

We don't always get to pick the soundtrack when we're having a haunting adolescent moment, but if you could choose the soundtrack to your life, what would be playing?

There are two solid approaches to this. First, you could list the songs that were actually playing during big moments in your life—your first slow dance with your high school crush, the song you played with your college roommates when you were getting ready to hit the town. You could tell us about the first record or CD you bought with your own money, or mention the albums that you wore out from constant play.

The second approach is to make a cohesive mixed tape by viewing your own storyline as if it were a movie, putting together a list of songs that evoke certain feelings but still flow when you play them together. Make a playlist or even a compilation you can link to from your blog.

78 | Go multimedia.

You know that little movie button on your digital camera? The one you've pushed twice, both times by accident? Try using it to create content. You can plan out a presentation, or just record a spontaneous moment.

The team at SkinnyCorp—makers of the Threadless tee you are probably wearing right now—posts videos of their office adventures (www.skinnycorp.com/video). My favorites include "Marmite Taste Off," "T-Shirt Gun Testing," and "Let's Have a Break Dance Party," pictured here.

skinnyPlayer

skinnyPlayer

79 | Say cheese.

I suspect you're already way ahead of me here, but if you don't already have a free Flickr account (www.flickr.com), you need one.

Flickr is Yahoo's photo-sharing service. It lets you organize, share, and print your photos, see photos from your friends, and participate in simple group projects by adding descriptive tags to images. Most importantly for our purposes, it gives you an easy interface for posting images to your blog.

After you've entered a little bit of information about your blog, you can load a photo to Flickr, hit the Blog This button above the photo, and then type in whatever text you'd like to appear in your post. I've found that Flickr makes it much more likely that I'll supplement a post with photos.

80 | Keep it in the family.

Great, great Aunt Betsy could go at any moment, and you have no idea about all that money she has secreted under her floorboards. Get to know the extended family a little better by using a blog to collect your family history online.

You can ask family members about their lives and then post their responses, or you can start a group blog. Give everyone a login, and post a new question every week. Ask about early memories, fondest moments with the family, or how everyone made it through difficult times.

Photos of family heirlooms go alongside the stories of where they came from and why they're precious. You can show us your family tree, create a section for everyone's wedding photos, or even plan the next reunion.

Phil Gregory (www.aperiodic.net/phil) created a moving tribute to his mother by scanning all of her handwritten recipe cards. Now everyone in the family, and on the Web, can enjoy her Christmas Greens.

5 Think Like a Writer

In the end, blogging is just writing. This chapter helps you think more like a writer and develop habits that will make you proud of your work.

81 | Exit the comfort zone.

Start saying yes. Tupperware party? Sounds like a swell time. Roller derby? Count me in. World jazz? Seriously? Uh, sure. The more you experience, the more you have to write about.

Seek out unusual opportunities and book them. Say yes to activities that ordinarily wouldn't seem appealing. A dubious evening may be worth the legendary post that comes out of it.

And who knows, you may develop a lasting interest in world jazz.

82 | Get it down.

How many times have you thought, "I should post about that," only to forget all about it by the time you're near a computer again?

Carry a notebook and pen with you. Always. Adopting this single habit will improve your posts tenfold. If a notebook sounds too cumbersome, write on the backs of business cards or index cards. You can discreetly record conversations, quick ideas, things you see in passing. If you do this consistently, you'll find that you're able to choose the best idea among many, rather than wracking your brain for one decent post.

83 | Start reading.

If you'd never read a novel, obviously you'd be at a pretty big disadvantage if you decided to write one. The same is true of blogging.

Reading lots of other blogs helps you develop your own well of ideas, and gives you an objective sense of how to write a post that interests others. Look for bloggers you'd like to emulate, and see who they link to in their blogrolls. Try to read someone new every day. Soon, you'll piece together a group of bloggers that helps keep you motivated to update your blog. Plus, you'll have great material to link to when you're going through a dry spell.

84 | Break the news.

You wake to the soothing sound of ocean waves outside your window. Unfortunately, you're in Nevada. You turn on the news and learn that the entire West Coast has broken off and floated out to sea. After a brief celebration at finding yourself the owner of beachfront property, you begin to search the Web for details.

Your blog can be an information repository during an historical event, especially one that's happening close to you. So, as long as you're looking for information, start recording findings for your readers. It not only helps keep everyone up to speed, it can be a valuable record of your experience of an event as it unfolds.

85 | Branch out.

Though it's generally a good idea to maintain your tone so that readers know what to expect, don't feel boxed in. Every once in a while, take your standard post and tweak it. If you're often light and sunny, an especially poignant post will resonate even more.

The most difficult part of this task could be figuring out how you're presenting yourself in the first place. When you reread your posts, you may be surprised to find that most of them are complaints, or that it's full of commentary on subjects that don't interest you as deeply as your posting habits would suggest. Find out who readers think you are, and offer another vantage.

86 | Use what you have.

Use your surroundings as a jumpstart. Flip through a stack of postcards, or go through the newspapers in the recycling bin. Turn to photo albums or your CD collection to bring up memories.

Sort through your personal papers, or just open the dictionary and find a word that you can build on. Any book on your shelf could be fuel for a post. After all, if someone else can write a hundred pages on a subject, surely you can come up with a hundred words.

87 | Do what you love.

Consider your passion. Could you make an entire blog about biking, digital cameras, relationships?

I've always heard successful people say that when you find the work you were meant to do, it doesn't feel like work. I never completely believed it, but I finally decided to try it. I asked myself, "What do I do when I want to relax?" I like to poke around at online stores.

I decided to start a shopping blog called Mighty Goods (www.mightygoods.com), and people immediately responded. It's won awards from all kinds of magazines, the ads on the site do well, and I've even had offers to write about shopping for others.

Choose a subject you're passionate about and consider devoting yourself to it. You may not want to be a professional blogger, but you're more likely to maintain your blog in the long term if you're posting about things you care about.

88 | Choose your company.

In one post you highlight the most tragic incidents in your childhood, in the next you outline ten steps for professional success. Who are you talking to here? Your friends, relatives, professional community, strangers you'd like to meet—all these folks are a potential audience, but you can't successfully talk to everyone at once.

Before you can figure out how and what to write, you have to decide whom you want to reach. Are your content and tone consistent with the audience you're looking to attract? Make a list of three things that would interest your ideal readers and write a post just for them.

89 | Inch your way there.

Let a project unfold over time. Ron Lutz (www.pbase.com/darter02/picture_a_day_for_a_year) decided to take a photo every day for a year and post them in the order he shot them. He stuck with it, and the result is 365 photos that catalog a year of his life and his learning curve as a photographer.

My slow-and-steady project is collecting portraits of my friends and loved ones:

90 | Keep it up.

You go a few days without posting, and then a couple of weeks, and pretty soon you have months of empty archives. Presto, your blog is stiff as a corpse. If you want to keep rigor mortis from setting in, you'll need to find a way to produce fresh content at least a couple times a week.

If you're having trouble posting regularly, try making it the first thing you do each day. For one month, post either immediately after you've woken up or at the very start of your workday. Things we shift to the end of our to do list have a tendency to drop off our radar. Put your site at the top of the list, and see what happens.

91 | Take up stalking.

Find a centrally located bench, and do some people watching. You can make conjectures about passersby, or just recount the highlights of what you observe. From my Mighty Girl blog:

> This couple is crossing the street on a cold Sunday morning. He's wearing a baggy sweatshirt, jeans, and a baseball cap. She's wearing a black halter top, dangling earrings, tight jeans, and high heels.
>
> - Wow. He's walking her home from last night.
>
> - They had a good night last night. That's why he's walking her home.
>
> - She's extra cute.
>
> - That's why he's walking her home.
>
> - He'd like for that to maybe happen again sometime, please.
>
> - Why didn't he offer her a sweatshirt or something?
>
> - He did. She's fine. Thanks though.
>
> - Look at how he's looking at her, he wants to keep her around.
>
> - If he were on his game, he would have dressed up a little so she wouldn't look so Saturday-night next to him.
>
> - That's why, when you shrink a sweater in the wash, you should keep it around.
>
> - For the tramps?
>
> - She's not a tramp. Tramps walk home alone.

92 | Look harder.

As our attention spans shorten and our patience follows suit, we miss the small good things that make life sweet. Why wait until something goes *bang* before you take notice? Once you start paying closer attention to everything around you, you'll come across found objects that inspire you.

Dean Allen (www.textism.com) made a "found alphabet" by photographing rural items that were shaped like letters. Rusted chain loops make the humps of the letter "B," a muddy boot stands in for a stoic "L," and the handles of an open pair of pruning shears form the walls of a "V." With a little reflection, you too can turn nothing into something.

93 | Share the joke.

When something makes you laugh, take note. Amusing incidents almost always translate into good posts. Here, a conversation with my roommates cracked me up:

Jenny: I've only ever gotten two tickets.

Me: Tell the speeding one.

J: It was bad.

M: What were you doing?

J: I was going 92 in a 55.

Rachel: Geez!

J: And I talked back to the cop.

M: Why?

J: He was just going on and on about how I could've killed someone. You know?

R: What did you say?

J: I said, "Just give me the ticket."

M: Whoa.

J: I was in a hurry.

M: Where were you going?

J: To yoga.

94 | Find like minds.

If you're blogging about a distinct topic, build a community or advance your profession by giving your opinion on new developments. Posting articles on the best ways to approach common problems draws readers who are interested in that topic.

Jeffrey Veen (www.veen.com/jeff) often posts about his work improving and simplifying large Web sites. Here's an excerpt from his post about a few new terms he'd learned while working on a project:

> Boil the Ocean *v.* Try to solve too many problems with an overambitious project, typically resulting in a complete failure. Many content management projects end up this way when attempting to port an entire organization's content, process, and workflow into one new, massive tool. "Look, just help the HR teams get their forms online. We don't need to boil the ocean with this."
>
> SUAC *v.* Acronym for "Shut Up and Color." How marketing and engineering departments often think (or wish) design should be done.
>
> S2BU *n.* Acronym for "Sucks To Be You." A page with an error message that communicates to the user that they are not authorized to continue an interaction. "If they aren't retired or over 55, they get an S2BU and we point them to the home page."

95 | Mine your media history.

You'd be terrified if you lost your computer. Security and productivity issues aside, you have no idea what's on the thing anymore.

Spend a few hours sorting through your files. Seek out stale goal sheets, unsent letters, pro and con lists for decisions long passed, class projects, photos you scanned in years ago, old footage of you dancing in the living room. How much of this stuff do you even remember making?

While you're at it, flip through the notebooks and journals sitting on your shelves. Pull out anything amusing, touching, or historically relevant to your life, and post it online.

96 | Lend us your ear.

You'll find that eavesdropping can dramatically enhance your blog content. Some of my best posts land in my lap while I'm commuting:

> Hat Guy is on the bus today, and he's feeling preachy. It's the noon bus, so most of the people on board are tourists headed into the city for a day of shopping. Hat Guy is making them gravely uncomfortable, which seems to make him happy. Here, a sampling of his insights:
>
> ON POVERTY
> The problem is, we got too many folks addicted to sleeping under the sky. Addicted. And then we offer them these itty bitty shelters. Let me ask you something. If you've got a great big house, why you gonna trade that for a little small house? Right?
>
> ON MARRIAGE
> Paul said, if you're a man, and you're hot to trot, you should get married. He didn't put any conditions on that. He didn't say, only to a woman! You have to marry a woman! No! He said, get married. And that's the end of that.

ON RELIGION

Bring out the religious stuff and the crowd goes dead.

ON TRAVEL

And for those of you who are tourists, this is San Francisco. You come here, you expect to have your mind blown wide open.

ON CIVIL RIGHTS

Does anyone think they might need an attorney in the next couple of minutes?

97 | Leave the house.

So, what's happening in your living room, buddy? Not much, huh? We can tell by how you haven't posted in a week.

Get up, dust yourself off, and grab your coat. Go spend a day in the world. It doesn't really matter what you do, as long as you do it outside the house. Take a book with you and stake out a coffee shop, ride the bus around town, go to an art show you've been meaning to see, and then let us know how it went. If you don't live, you can hardly expect anyone to read about your life, now can you?

98 | Gripe.

Friends who start dating and stop calling, waiters who ignore repeated requests for water, people who let the door close in your face, the project manager who stretches a fifteen-minute meeting to an hour by virtue of his or her idiocy—vent your pet peeves online and you may find that your annoyance gives your post a little punch. From Mighty Girl:

> When a cat misbehaves you squirt a light mist of water in his face so he learns not to do something again. A societal equivalent would be so satisfying. When the girl at the coffee shop orders "a caramel frappucino with semi-dry foam," you could just tap her on the nose with a rolled up magazine and say, "NO, Tiffany! Bad. NO."

99 | Obsess.

Photograph everywhere you go for a week, note everything you buy for a month, record each outfit you wear for a year. Mildly (or majorly) obsessive posts are so much more illuminating than a snippet here and there.

Geoff Badner (www.geoffbadner.com/blog) took a photo of everything he ate for a week and published the results as a photo essay for The Morning News (www.themorningnews.org/archives/stories/appetite). His most appealing photos are of the incidental snacks most people would never record.

Join him for Pringles in front of the TV, a handful of Skittles on an airplane, a pan full of popcorn on the stoop. Next best thing to mooching.

100 | Just write.

How many people have visited your site today? More than yesterday? No! Less! Is that because it's only 8 a.m.? Or is it because people hate that last post you wrote? They definitely hate it. You should take it down. But who do these people think they are? You can write whatever you want! Who are they to decide whether your work has merit? Still, maybe you should take it down.

Whoa there. Get yourself a soothing cup of herbal tea, and think about why you're doing this. Most people who blog do not have many readers. And by "most," I mean that the *vast majority* of bloggers are writing for their friends and family. If your only motivation is to write for an audience, you may find it tough to maintain the moderate but consistent pace you need to earn that audience.

Frankly, providing a steady stream of content for a few years is one of the only sure ways to build traffic. That means you'll need more profound motivation than building a readership. You'll need to love what you're writing about.

So take a breath, back away from the stats, and make your own list of things that make you want to write. Post about each and every one, and then leave the keyboard in peace.

Index

Q

R

S

About the Author

Margaret Mason lives with her husband in San Francisco. Her shopping blog, Mighty Goods, was named #1 shopping site by both *Business Week* and *Forbes.* Since 2000, her personal site, Mighty Girl, has drawn thousands of readers each day. Maggie is the former Managing Editor of CMP Media's *Web Techniques* magazine, and has been a professional writer and editor for over a decade. Her work has appeared in *The New York Times,* and she is a fashion and etiquette columnist for The Morning News, a New York-based Web magazine. Maggie also blogs professionally for *ReadyMade* magazine. She is a sought-after speaker and an expert on lifestyle topics. Maggie has been interviewed by *The New York Times, Elle,* the *San Francisco Chronicle,* and *The San Jose Mercury News,* among others.